THE
Regency
GUIDE TO
Romance

A Pocket Companion to Love and Courtship

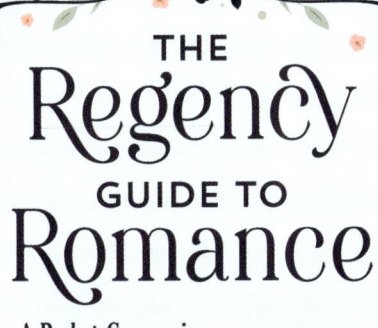

Francis Nightingale

summersdale

THE REGENCY GUIDE TO ROMANCE

Copyright © Octopus Publishing Group Limited, 2025

All rights reserved.

Text by Abigail McMahon

No part of this book may be reproduced by any means, nor transmitted, nor translated into a machine language, without the written permission of the publishers.

Condition of Sale
This book is sold subject to the condition that it shall not, by way of trade or otherwise, be lent, resold, hired out or otherwise circulated in any form of binding or cover other than that in which it is published and without a similar condition including this condition being imposed on the subsequent purchaser.

An Hachette UK Company
www.hachette.co.uk

Summersdale Publishers
Part of Octopus Publishing Group Limited
Carmelite House
50 Victoria Embankment
LONDON
EC4Y 0DZ
UK

This FSC® label means that materials and other controlled sources used for the product have been responsibly sourced

www.summersdale.com

The authorized representative in the EEA is Hachette Ireland, 8 Castlecourt Centre, Dublin 15, D15 XTP3, Ireland (email: info@hbgi.ie)

Printed and bound in China

ISBN: 978-1-83799-728-2
eISBN: 978-1-83799-729-9

Substantial discounts on bulk quantities of Summersdale books are available to corporations, professional associations and other organizations. For details contact general enquiries: telephone: +44 (0) 1243 771107 or email: enquiries@summersdale.com.

CONTENTS

Introduction
4

Part One
Love, Lust and Longing
5

Part Two
Hearts Most Broken
44

Part Three
Proposals and Promises
85

Conclusion
125

INTRODUCTION

Welcome, reader, to love. With this compendium in hand, you may walk love's path. The sage advice within these pages will guide you deftly past unwanted suitors, purposefully through the maze of social mores and directly into the arms of your heart's desire. From those first flutterings of love and pangs of heartbreak, to the delight and delirium of forming a relationship, these hints and tips will help you comport yourself with befitting dignity. So sally forth, love bravely and live boldly!

Part One
Love, Lust and Longing

Oh, happy news! Having taken a few turns around the ballroom, your eyes have alighted upon a most dashing figure. Perhaps your heart beats with devotion, perhaps your body trembles with… we shall not linger on that topic. Instead, let us address that most confounding question: what to do next? Should you speak, and in speaking risk an uncivil rejection? Or, stay strong, silent and… single?

The following pages will give you a hint as to how best to convey your feelings to the object of your fascination, in a manner most becoming and not at all addled. We provide vignettes to enlighten every mind, from ardent hunters on the marriage mart to those merely hoping to get up a flirt before the season ends.

CONTRIVING TO CONVERSE

Many people appear to be very fetching from across a ballroom, or with the use of an Instagram filter, but their attraction withers altogether when exposed to conversation. Increase the fluttering of your butterflies or put them to rest altogether with these dazzling conversation starters:

"Do you enjoy a rubber?" You are of course enquiring if they are partial to a game of whist, rather than their favourite pencil topper or preferred method of contraception.

"Would you care for a glass of ratafia?" This is a sweetened liquor – not to be confused with the straw raffia or the material taffeta.

Love rules the court, the camp, the grove, and men below, and the saints above; for love is heaven, and heaven is love.

SIR WALTER SCOTT,
THE LAY OF THE LAST MINSTREL

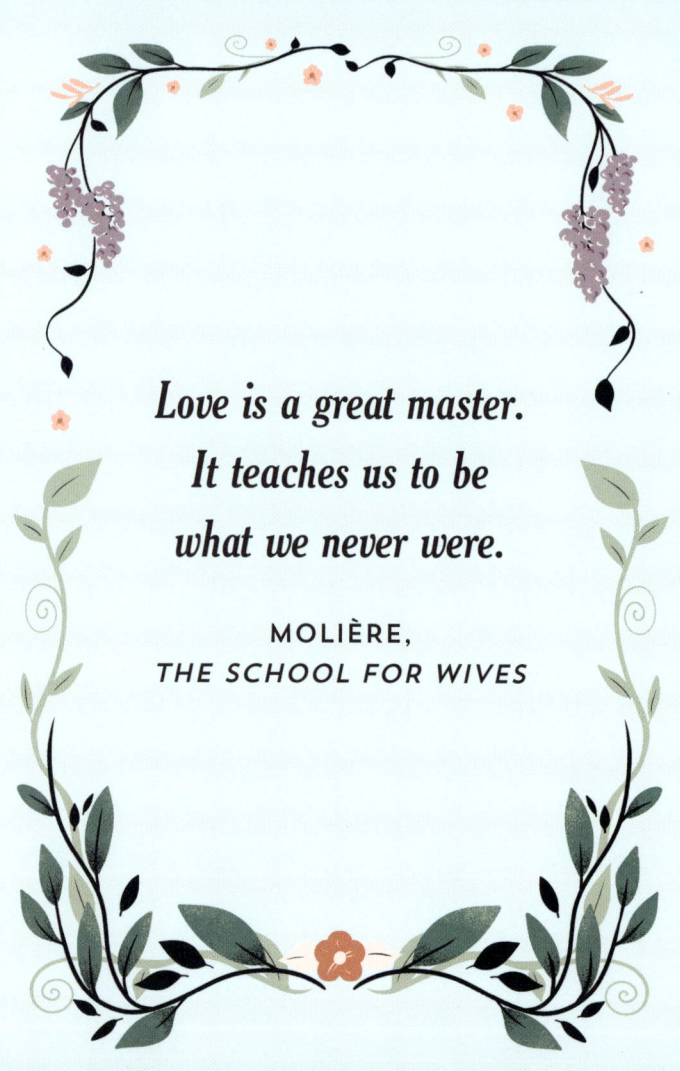

*Love is a great master.
It teaches us to be
what we never were.*

MOLIÈRE,
THE SCHOOL FOR WIVES

TABLE MANNERS

It must be supposed that readers have mastered the niceties of dinner parties and are not so fresh from the schoolroom that they cannot tell the epergne from the chafing dish. Instead, we offer the lightest refreshment for those wishing to particularly impress certain fellow diners:

- ♥ One must converse with one's neighbours, even when one has been disappointed by the seating arrangement.

- ♥ One must not lean over or around for dishes or new conversational partners. We are not a sapling in the breeze.

- ♥ One must accept the soup course, even if one does not care for the flavour.

- ♥ One must not slurp the soup, and by no means complete any actions associated with dipping, dunking or scooping.

LOVE IN THE PUMP ROOMS

Falling in love has many fashions, as is the case with all matters of society. A hopeful miss may have once found love in the pump rooms – that delightful daytime place to meet with the best of society, converse and take the spa waters. We have heard that in these modern times there are now rooms where people gather to pump iron, but that is another, altogether sweatier and far less romantic affair. Perhaps best avoided.

*If I could but know his heart,
everything would become easy.*

JANE AUSTEN,
SENSE AND SENSIBILITY

SECURING AN INTRODUCTION

An introduction made in a ballroom is sufficient for a lady and a gentleman to dance together on that happy occasion. It does not, however, hold any power outside of the ballroom. Simply put, Regency manners dictate that what happens in the ballroom must certainly stay in the ballroom, unless the lady wishes for it to be otherwise.

This is, of course, the most sensible course of action. A lady might make the acquaintance of a gentleman in the flickering light of a dance floor that she may not wish to pursue in the steadfast light of day.

MAY I INTRODUCE YOU?

There will be introductions that one is hopeful – even desirous – of receiving. After all, many love-smitten souls have stepped nimbly from first dance to wedding dance. But who may issue that coveted first introduction?

According to Regency etiquette, when attending a private ball, the hostess may introduce gentlemen to ladies. When attending a public ball, the Master of Ceremonies may introduce gentlemen to ladies. A common acquaintance may introduce two amenable parties on any occasion should the lady be agreeable.

At no point may a gentleman be considered introduced to a lady if he has slid into her DMs. Even if the lady, in a moment of weakness, has replied.

A RAKE'S ENTRANCE

One must always be on the lookout for a rake: a person with a reputation for immoral behaviour and fraternization. It may be true that sometimes true love enters one's life windswept and on horseback. Certainly, they may be silver-tongued and quick-witted, a friend to all, except those who have sadly wronged them. And indeed, they may also be virtually in possession of a competent fortune, were it not for circumstances quite beyond their ability to rectify. However, if this paragon spends as much time making you weep for their misfortune as they do provoking delighted laughter, they may more likely be a rake.

BUT TO SEE HER WAS
TO LOVE HER;
LOVE BUT HER,
AND LOVE FOREVER.

ROBERT BURNS,
"AE FOND KISS"

THE CUT

Although some suitors are destined to be eternal tenants of your heart, some are far more suited to a six-month rolling contract with *no* option for renewal. Only a pudding-head would ignore the direction to find a roost in some other worthy person's heart, but we regret to say that the world is plagued by pudding-heads.

Here are two routes you may take in order to encourage a reluctant evictee to move on:

The Cut Indirect

For when you still have recourse to be civil. You reply to no missives, reject all invites and certainly have no interest in discussing the matter any further. In public you model yourself after your least friendly colleague – you may exchange a nod, but you by no means enquire after their health, wealth or weekend plans.

The Cut Direct

A person of quality is never rude. Your motto, when plagued by an odiously ill-mannered former suitor who ignores all pleas to be let alone, should be to block, block, block. That is, block their number, block their socials and block their email too. After all, *they* may wish to say such nonsense, but *you* are under no circumstances required to listen.

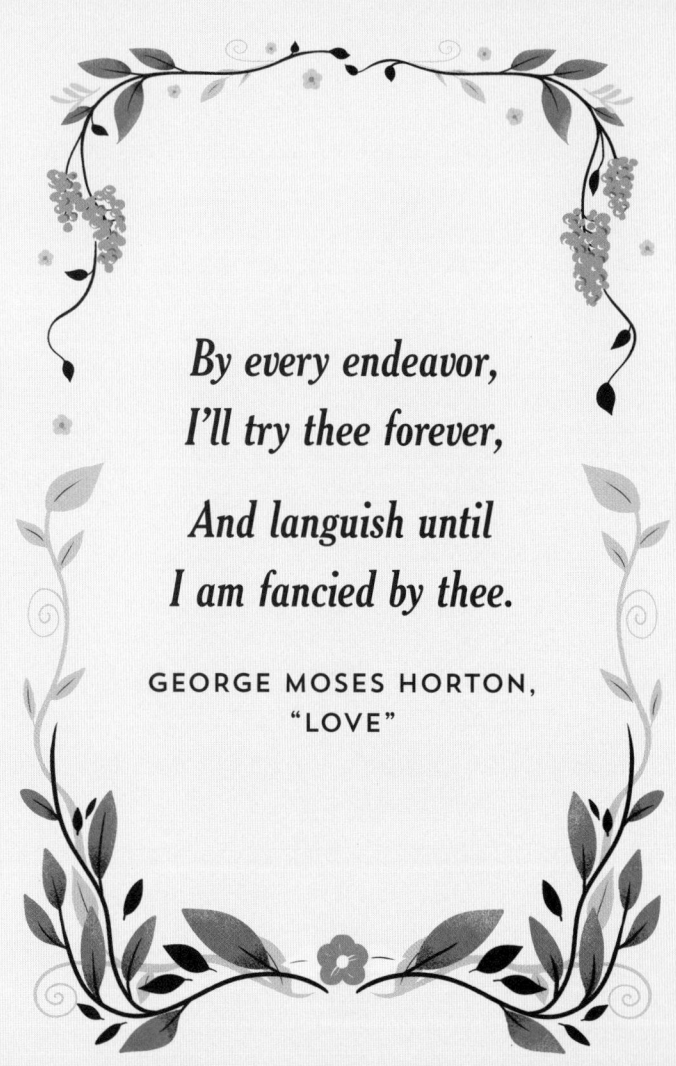

*By every endeavor,
I'll try thee forever,*

*And languish until
I am fancied by thee.*

GEORGE MOSES HORTON,
"LOVE"

PROMENADING

A ball is a very merry meeting place indeed, but it is not the only forum for the marriage mart. Consider fashionable parks and seaside promenades. There are quite as many ladies peeping from under their bonnets, or glancing up from their phones, at finely turned-out calves as there are gentlemen bowing gallantly to every female acquaintance with whom they have the slightest familiarity.

A lady on the lookout for love might be advised to wear the coat which most becomes her. In turn, the hopeful gentleman should advise his valet that his shirt points should be as high and starched as is in his power.

FINDING LOVE IN FRIENDSHIP'S GARDEN

Love does not always arrive in the guise of a tall stranger. It may indeed bloom from the fertile earth of friendship. Plucking this blossom requires a soft hand, for you do not wish to disturb the soil and place yourself permanently in the "friend zone".

To those inexperienced in the cycle of love and friendship, know that neither are bound to any particular season. A fresh and springlike connection and a cosy autumnal intimacy could both give way to love.

We have tortured our metaphor for long enough. A closing hint: one should never underestimate the power of a short walk and a gentle confession.

All thoughts, all passions, all delights, Whatever stirs this mortal frame, All are but ministers of Love.

SAMUEL TAYLOR COLERIDGE, "LOVE"

SURE STEPS TO LOVE

As Austen once proclaimed, dancing is a sure step to love. Let us review society's favoured dances to ensure it is not a sure step to scandal.

Quadrille

Undoubtedly a fashionable dance, but not one beyond the bounds of conventional taste. Couples form a larger party and trip pleasingly across the floor to genteel music. The steps are intricate, and the compositions many, so this dance is not for the weak of constitution or memory.

Waltz

As to be expected of a dance from the continent, this is quite beyond the pale: a couple, arranged but a breath apart, hands resting upon each other's person. Some of the more well-starched members of society are practically overcome by the swoons just to witness it.

Twerking

Let others write of such things, for we cannot.

HEALTH AND WELL-BEING

Having emerged from the heavily powdered and patched era of our poor, deluded mamas, we Regency lovers are in our clean beauty era. One must take utmost care of one's skin to catch the eye of our would-be suitors. These remedies and preparations are suggested by the foremost thinkers of the nineteenth century, although one must always defer to the recommendations of the modern medical practitioner.

A Modest Bath

This bath imitates the effects of Queen Cleopatra's bath of asses' milk:

- ♥ Four ounces peeled almonds
- ♥ One pound pineapple kernels
- ♥ One pound elecampane
- ♥ Ten handfuls linseed

- ♥ One ounce marsh mallow petals
- ♥ One ounce white lily petals

Reduce ingredients to a paste through a good application of strength and a heavy object. Stuff several small bags with the paste and place in your bath, until it becomes milky. If the above ingredients are difficult to procure, then a trip to your local chemist should suffice. Simply ask them for "bath bombs".

🌿 CALLING ROUND 🌿

According to Regency etiquette, a gentleman should always be the first to call on a lady, but a lady may call on another gentlewoman of her acquaintance. Unless the two are intimate friends, the visit should take place as a "morning call". Despite the name, these take place in the afternoon. On receiving a calling card from her visitor, the lady will inform her servants as to whether she is at home to callers. A lady may be in her home but tell visitors she is not at home. The modern-day version of this is of course observing callers through our video doorbell cameras and deciding if we are "home" to receive them. If one is at home to visitors, a visit is no more than a quarter of an hour. Within several days, this visit should be returned and these rituals repeated. What a happy way to spend our time.

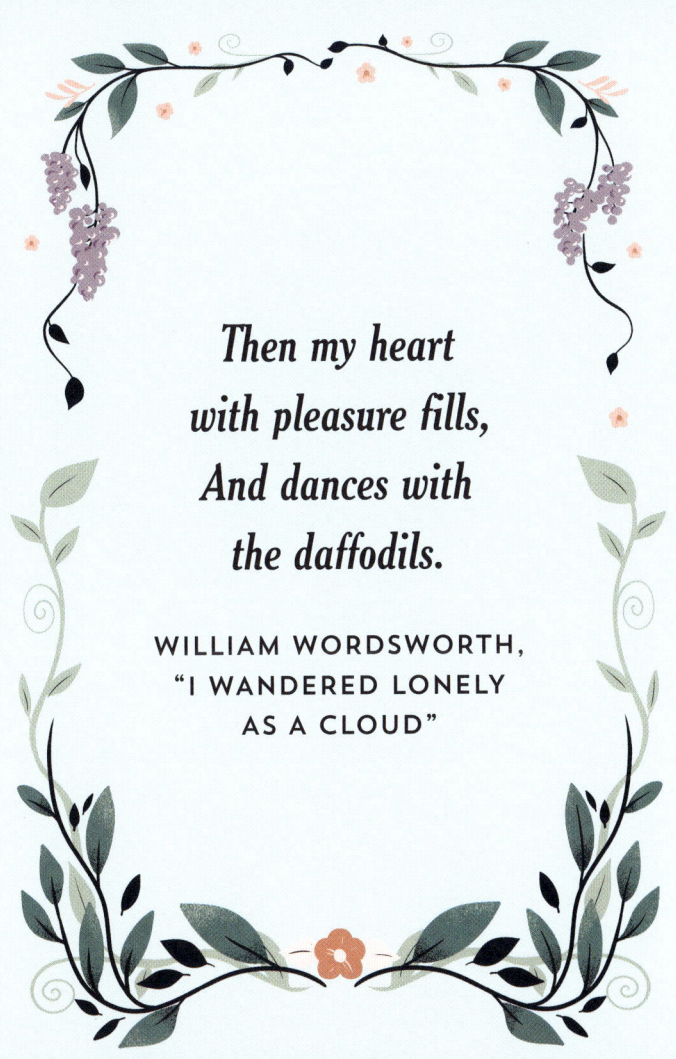

Sweet, sweet is the greeting of eyes, And sweet is the voice in its greeting.

JOHN KEATS,
"SWEET, SWEET IS THE
GREETING OF EYES"

ITEMS TO BE DROPP'D

You may be sure that the striking trim of your gown would enchant anyone who gazed upon it. You must, then, turn the gaze of those you wish to be enchanted upon it. Here is a word on those items that may be dropp'd. In all cases, check for muddy puddles before you do so.

- A single glove (of a pair that can survive a stain).

- Your reticule (emptied of all you would not wish to lose).

- Your fan (unless battery powered, as this may end in disaster if said item lands on a foot; borrow your sister's if you would fear to lose your own).

- Your most accomplished piece of needlework (suitable for house parties only).

- A book/e-reader (should your would-be suitor appreciate one who reads).

LOVE AND ENMITY

Is it possible that the most odious person you know could one day become the dearest? That depends entirely on the nature of your disgust with them and, it must be said, the size of their estate. A taciturn person may yet show you an aspect of their character that is kind, witty, or so very, very wealthy. It may be that a nattering person, who appears foolish with every sixth sentence, has stores of wisdom hidden away. Besides, they would have informed you of their income within minutes of you having met.

In every province, the chief occupations, in order of importance, are lovemaking, malicious gossip and talking nonsense.

VOLTAIRE, *CANDIDE*

A LETTER TO A RIVAL IN LOVE

On occasion, the journey through the marriage mart has all the discomfort of crossing a country road in a carriage. Here, we offer the reader a phrase or two that may be employed upon discovering a friend has made a rather too intimate connection with someone you yourself had thought to be down the road to marriage with.

Dearest Friend,

I cannot express my delight in hearing you have made the acquaintance of our dear Mr/Miss/Mx———. I assure you, you hardly need tell me how well they wear their form-fitting breeches/dart across the dance floor/make convivial conversation with our wretched cousin. I am quite aware of their manifold charms.

My dear sister had already informed me of the charming picnic/raucous house party/country ramble where you spent so much time tête-à-tête. It so cheers me to hear that two of my dearest friends have grown so close.

Aren't they simply the kindest creature? I can just picture the charity of their response when you told them of your family's utter destitution/multitude of broken engagements/disdain for tasteful dress.

Write to me soon and often.

Your faithful servant

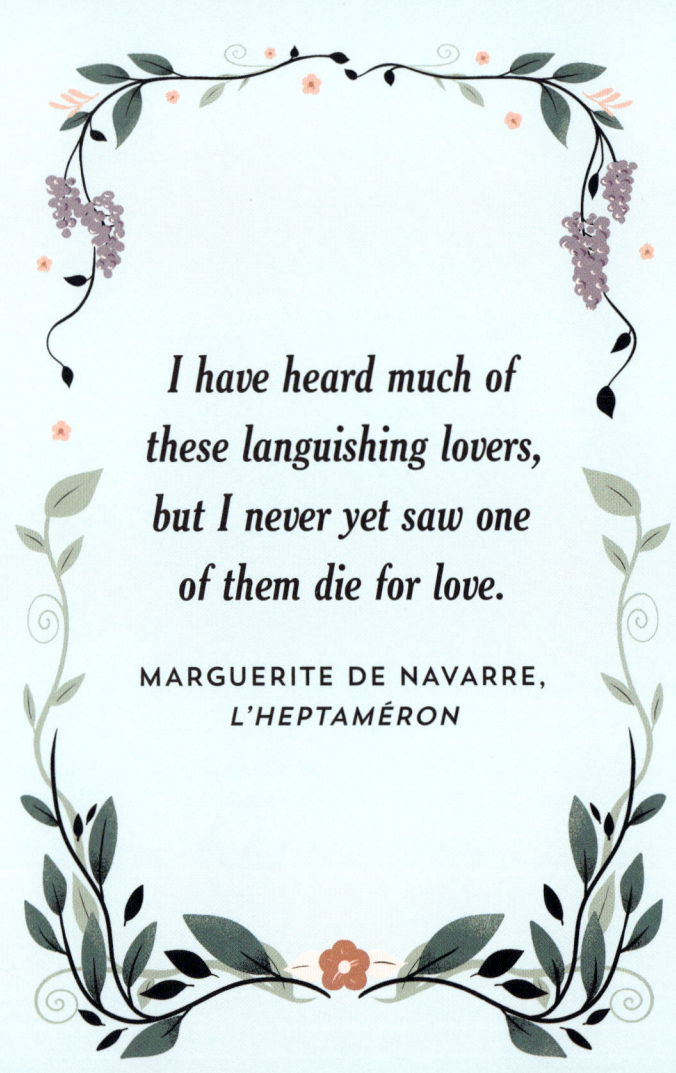

I have heard much of these languishing lovers, but I never yet saw one of them die for love.

MARGUERITE DE NAVARRE,
L'HEPTAMÉRON

MATCHMAKING

Is it better to go about your daily business and hope that you will one day encounter the one person who can complete your happiness? Or should you find it more pleasing – and a great deal more convenient – to make yourself known to potential suitors via a matchmaking app?

We believe it is a matter of personal taste – after all, we appear to our best advantage when we are easy in our environment. However, a great many matchmaking mamas would disagree. They would insist you appear at every ball and feature on every app, lest her closest friend's ungainly daughter be married before you.

DIVERTING UNWELCOME ATTENTION

Regency ladies are generally known to employ mysterious arts in order to appear to their best advantage. They have also mastered another discipline, practised rather more furtively: the art of repulsing the attention of an unwanted suitor without disgusting society in general.

Clumsy Dancing

You may be able to distract a deficient suitor from the pangs in their heart by offering them plentiful pangs of the foot. Even someone very much on their way to being in love might find that a barrage of wildly swinging elbows and misplaced knees quells their ardour.

Appearing Foolish

This approach has a pleasing versatility that can be adapted to suit your individual character. In one instance there is a giggling, nattering sort of foolishness which smothers the conversation in incomprehension. In another instance, there is a blinking, slack-mouthed sort of foolishness which drowns any conversation in silence.

Appearing Over-Accomplished

It is difficult to create a daringly romantic scene if you are always preoccupied by your dancing master, or watercolour master, or harpsichord master – or indeed any persons with half of a skill or more.

Love and scandal are the best sweeteners of tea.

HENRY FIELDING,
LOVE IN SEVERAL MASQUES

COMMITTING YOUR SENTIMENTS TO PAPER

It is quite natural for lovebirds to fill those dreary hours apart with billets overflowing with adoring words. After all, they are quite determined to be together forever. And indeed, if it were not for those two natural enemies of true love – shipwrecks and beautiful heiresses – they would be. Until these threats are exterminated, it is not wise for lovers to overextend themselves in ink. Be canny and keep your most passionate sentiments to fervent whispers in the gardens or use "disappearing messages" on your favourite messaging app.

GETTING AN UNFORTUNATE HEAD COLD

A head cold is the unhappy companion of a coveted invitation. Just when a Regency lady is engaged to attend a picnic or the opera, or take a tour of the countryside with a most attractive companion, she is stricken by a head cold. Do not venture out regardless. If music be the food of love, wretched coughing and sniffing must certainly be its poison. While a surgical mask draws attention to the eyes and adds mystery, it cannot disguise the harrumphing and spluttering within. And do not fret that your absence will dash all hopes of deepening your connection. After all, absence makes the heart grow fonder.

THE PLEASURE OF LOVE IS IN LOVING.

FRANÇOIS DE LA ROCHEFOUCAULD,
REFLECTIONS

🌿 FIVE OCCASIONS 🌿
ONE MIGHT SWOON

A swoon is not always acceptable, but is sometimes inevitable.

1. When a suitor helps one down from a carriage.
2. Upon being saved from brigands by a handsome stranger.
3. After reading a romantic missive.
4. When one's attractive frenemy emerges from the lake.
5. Upon seeing a suitor's extensive grounds.

THE FLIRTATION STYLES OF A REGENCY HERO(INE)

Your heart has found its object. Now, you must select which hero(ine) you shall imitate when attempting to fix your interest.

Deep Feeler

You tremble with passion, not unlike a Chihuahua *sans* coat. Every other sentence spoken is a quotation from a great poet.

Wallflower

You say nothing. The object of your affection will notice you, once they have noticed every other potential conquest of the ton.

Acerbic Flirter

You simply insult them until they have fallen deeply in love with you.

Part Two
Hearts Most Broken

It is one of life's inevitabilities that most people must be disappointed in love. Only the luckiest, or the loneliest, escape that fate. Perhaps, for you, the time has come. The letter breaking off the connection has arrived. The cut direct has been delivered. Your heart may be rent entirely in two or it may be merely bruised. Regardless, you may take the following pages as the physick you require. Some are light cures for light ailments, others are remedies for the sorely used heart.

~ TÊTE-À-TÊTE ~

It is unlikely, if not impossible, that you will be able to avoid your former lover in polite society. It is our belief that you should not try. Rather, at your next public engagement, endeavour to place yourself near to your former love's worst relative. Even the highest paragon has an abhorrent aunt or priggish cousin. Spend the evening in their company and indeed, you may find your unwanted ardour somewhat dampened. You have no more reason to fear an uncomfortable country holiday with *that* person.

A LITTLE KINDNESS

Would you not be kind to a broken-hearted individual, should you encounter them during your daily merriment? You would not pass comment on their eyes, which are a little red from crying, or their outfit, which is somewhat dishevelled. You would not make them the object of fun, should their witty retorts come a little slower one evening. Why, that broken-hearted individual is you! In this trying time, extend to yourself the same generosity of spirit as you would any other person who has been crossed in love.

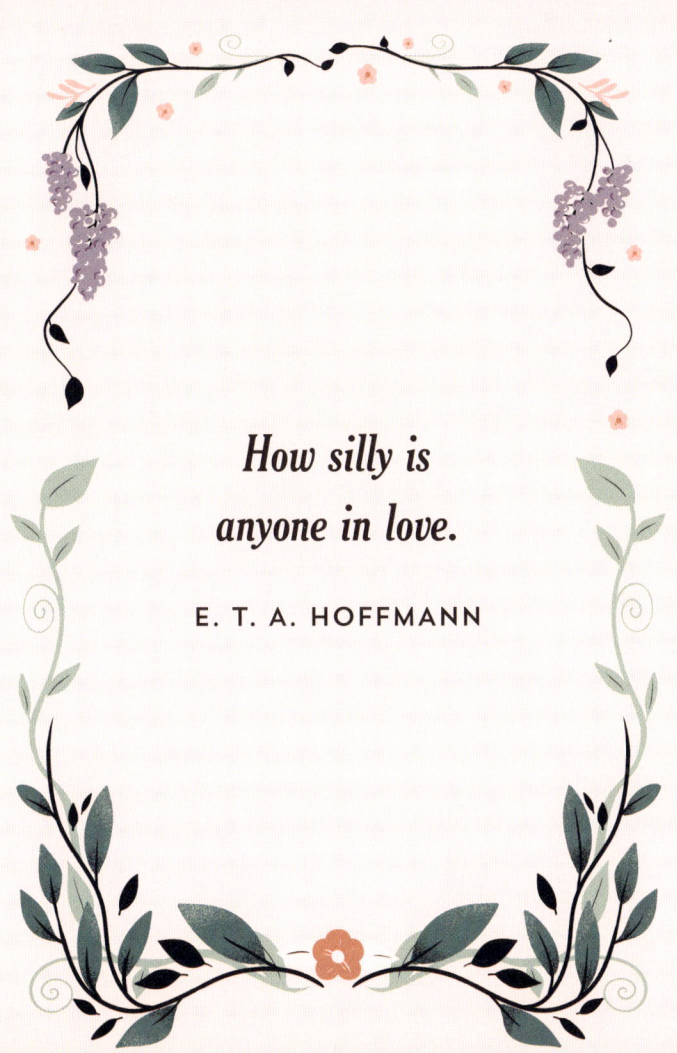

How silly is anyone in love.

E. T. A. HOFFMANN

FIVE REMEDIES FOR WOUNDED HEARTS

For jilted lovers who know they ought not to feel so sad but do, nonetheless, feel hopelessly mournful, try these remedies:

1. Sob into upholstery.
2. Purchase a fascinating hat.
3. Enjoy one night of shocking gaiety, followed by two days of the headache.
4. Take the waters in Bath, England.
5. Contrive to be introduced to a charming stranger.

BURNING THE LETTERS

In Regency etiquette, it is customary, upon breaking off a connection, for the gentleman to return any written communications exchanged between the two parties. Do not linger over the words you wrote when you were more disposed to affection. The author of those letters is now unknown to the reader.

Look to fresh beginnings. Burn the letters. However, if your missives are stored upon your smart device, do not burn that. A simple deletion – or if you feel the case is truly serious, block – will suffice. You will write new letters, just as you will find new love.

TAKE TO YOUR BED

There really cannot be too much praise given to the delicate art of taking to your bed. Retiring to your room will not suffice. It is far too solitary an activity. Taking to your bed must necessarily be a communal pastime. Encourage your household to partake in your healthy bout of theatrical misery.

Take Ill During Mealtime

It matters not when you first received the news of your heartbreak. Put off all thoughts of your pain until your household is gathered. Mealtimes are generally found to be the best time for this.

Collapse from Standing

Tragedy may turn to comedy if one merely slips sideways from their chair. Stand and weakly, but clearly, say "oh!" Fall, endeavouring to cushion your head on your arms.

Drape Yourself in Fabrics

Layers of fabric may enhance your pathetic fluttering. Sleepwear is a must; a dressing gown/onesie will enhance the look, and a large handkerchief is essential for dabbing weakly at your face.

A HOLIDAY FOR ONE'S HEART

To where should you retreat to nurse your broken heart?

The Country

This locale has plenty to offer the heartbroken, especially for those inclined to exorcize their pain through the means of exercise. Tromp through the mud and rain until all thoughts of your previous *amor* are quite gone, and the local gentry are quite astonished.

Bath

The only thing that leaves a worse taste in your mouth than disappointment in love is the sulphuric water of the fashionable resort town, Bath, England. Join polite society and enjoy a glassful of the spring waters – your distress will move swiftly from your heart to your stomach.

Brighton

Who knows in whose company one may find oneself, when among the gaiety of Brighton. This English seaside town is home to all walks of life... The militia. A prince. Scandalous actresses. One may well dance until one's shoes are in a sorrier state than one's heart.

London

There are likely as many eligible bachelors in London as there are houses. Recall, when one door closes, another opens. Situate yourself where you may encounter the most doors.

 ALL IS FAIR

Let us imagine a fitting revenge for your ex suitor. It will, of course, remain but a figment of our imagination. Of course. Perhaps they would…

- ♥ Trip over their own feet at the next ball.
- ♥ Be the subject of a shameful gossip rag.
- ♥ Have their fiancé/e elope… without them!
- ♥ Wear their hair in an embarrassingly outdated fashion.

O Love! who bewailest

The frailty of all things here,

Why choose you the frailest

*For your cradle, your home,
and your bier?*

PERCY BYSSHE SHELLEY,
"WHEN THE LAMP IS SHATTERED"

A GENTEEL SCANDAL

After experiencing a disappointment in love, it is quite a natural impulse to become inclined to a little scandal. A person who causes too much scandal may become quite unwelcome in polite society, but a little light scandal offers excellent refreshment to the spirits.

Dampen Your Skirts

It is a common practice among the more daring of the ton to lightly dampen their petticoats, though this is frowned upon by the more respectable. We neither recommend nor condemn, only note that dampened skirts show off a graceful figure.

Attend Vauxhall Pleasure Gardens... *at Night*

Flickering torchlight, beguiling music and a heady mix of companionship from all strata of society. Certainly, some corners of the maze are said to be a little too shadowed to be quite proper. But if that is true, then they must also be too shadowy for prying eyes to spy who roams them.

Dance the Waltz

The novelist Sophie von La Roche has described the waltz as an "indecent whirling-dance of the Germans", a view which is certainly taken by the gossiping mamas of polite society.

I have love in me the likes of which you can scarcely imagine.

MARY SHELLEY,
FRANKENSTEIN

NOT AT HOME TO CALLERS

Why does it seem that every third cousin, childhood friend and distant acquaintance takes it into their head to pay a call or issue invitations just as heartbreak has its grips on the home? For some these are welcome distractions, especially if their social circle was broken alongside their heart. For others, they provide unwelcome chatter, causing their head to ache.

If your sympathies lie with the latter, do not be afraid to retreat from society for a time. Instruct your staff that you are not at home to visitors. If you do not have staff, perhaps send a missive to your closest friends, advising them of your temporary reclusion.

༶ A MAXIM FOR ༶ CONSOLING SISTERS

Sisters are especially prone to heartache. The temptation is to speak one's truth on the cad who discarded a very beloved sister. Refrain. She may need a sweeter tonic for her pain.

Do not say, Sister, I am relieved that I no longer have to suffer through long evenings with your pea-goose of a suitor. I sincerely hope the next lover your heart alights upon may not be such a gudgeon.

Do say, Sister, let us do whatever may lift your spirits. If you wish to talk, we shall have a comfortable coze. If you wish to be silent, not a word will cross our lips.

BE CAUTIOUS IN HOW YOU BESTOW YOUR HEART

There can be no objection to a *flirtation*, in the wake of a ruined relationship. But beware of being carried away by the delight in your new beau's difference. What is at first refreshing – the way they laugh when the other would stay silent, that their tastes run to beer while the other preferred wine – is altogether too flimsy to act as a foundation for a lifelong connection. You should not shutter your heart, but neither should you advertise a vacancy.

LOVE AND FRIENDSHIP

Poets like to write extensively of lost love. We do not object too strenuously; after all, they must write of *something* and their pen appears incapable of enlarging on happier topics. Where objection can be found is in the idea that the heartbroken now faces a form of destitution.

Anyone who has friends and family is still in possession of a great wealth. They are loved dearly. Now, in this time of need, they should spend some of that currency by spending time with the people who love them most.

*The heart will break,
but broken live on.*

LORD BYRON, *DON JUAN*

 A LITERARY ESCAPE

Heart sickness can infect other aspects of your life. The afflicted finds themselves sick of walking the same old walks, attending the same old parties and dancing the same old dances. For a short period of time, while the clouds are descended, everything seems so utterly, utterly mundane.

A remedy can be found within these pages. The prescription is such: seek out and read books, or binge your favourite series. Find stories that send you to roam in distant, fantastical lands, that you may speak to unfamiliar people and learn histories unlike our own. There can be no better escape than that offered by a story.

HOW TO BE NONCHALANT WHEN MEETING AN EX SUITOR

It is commonly known that the very minute one begins to feel as though the weight of a painful breakup has been lifted is just the moment that same ex rounds the corner.

You may choose to take one of these actions:

1. Look fixedly in another direction.
2. Laugh hysterically, but only if with a companion.
3. Recall that you urgently require a new trim for your bonnet and run into the nearest dressmakers.
4. Nod at them with icy courtesy.
5. Fall into a swoon.

SPEECHES TO CONVINCE MISGUIDED FRIENDS

There comes a time in the recovery from heartsickness that resuming normal life holds every appeal in the world. After one has consumed their own weight in cake, moped in every corner of the house and stood windswept on every bluff in the county, running errands again is quite within one's power, and interest.

If only one's well-meaning friends realized this! Instead, they continue to treat one with a delicacy that becomes quite tedious. Repel their kindly meant overtures with these decisive postulations.

*"I am quite capable of attending
a ball, Cousin. Indeed, if I do not,
I shall be devastated by boredom!"*

*"I am feeling quite my old self. Which,
by the by, is how I have felt the last
dozen times you have asked."*

*"I have no need to suddenly turn round
to see a perfect puppy. Like you, I have
already seen that my ex stands across the
street, and, unlike you, I am unmoved."*

BECOME (MORE) ACCOMPLISHED

Time is considered an enemy by the broken-hearted. Hours that were once filled with dancing and laughing are now empty. To the contrary, to have a great deal of time and nothing to spend it on is of great value. Gift it back to yourself. Just think, with all these hours available for instruction and practice you could become a master of the pianoforte, a mountaineer of great daring or your county's foremost scholar of historical artefacts. You could lead intellectual debate at a coffee shop, or simply begin to take yourself for tea once a week to become reacquainted with yourself.

*Ah, lips that say one thing,
while the heart thinks another.*

ALEXANDRE DUMAS,
THE COUNT OF MONTE CRISTO

IF I CANNOT INSPIRE LOVE, I WILL CAUSE FEAR.

MARY SHELLEY, *FRANKENSTEIN*

A TASTE OF DANGER

Perhaps, in the wake of disappointed love, you have no appetite for worthy self-improvement. Instead, you would like to feel your heart beating so fast that it skips a beat once more. Try your hand at these restoratively thrilling activities to achieve your aim:

- Engage in a carriage race through the streets of the city.
- Disagree with the formidable Lord/Lady (insert name here), loudly and in public.
- Dance with a confirmed rake.
- Start a feud with the most vicious member of the ton.
- Save a puppy or young urchin from an oncoming hackney carriage.

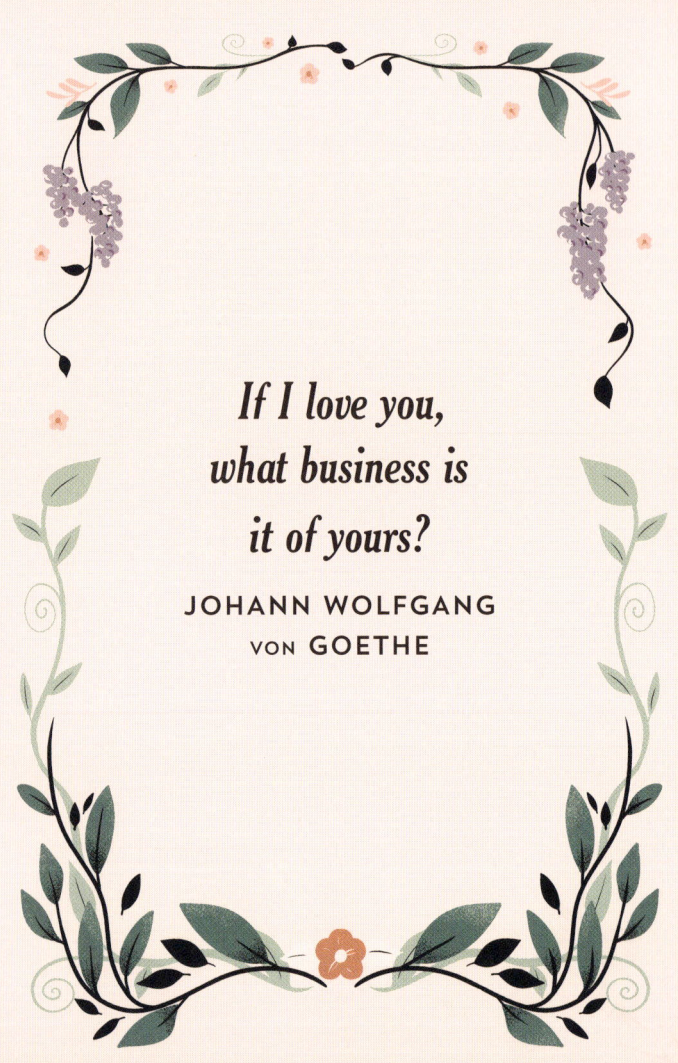

If I love you, what business is it of yours?

—JOHANN WOLFGANG VON GOETHE

But tell of days in goodness spent, A mind at peace with all below, A heart whose love is innocent!

LORD BYRON,
"SHE WALKS IN BEAUTY"

CLEANSING THE PALATE

A gentle flirtation is just the thing to remind the broken-hearted of all the most pleasant aspects of love, without exposing them to the dangers of shattering their heart for a second time. Why not spark a flirtation with one of the following:

The Rake

The village wise woman will often recommend the hair of the dog that bit you as a cure. Why not let a rake cure the condition that was a rake's doing? Only beware you do not get bitten a second time.

The Soldier

A merrymaking man, and one who has the athleticism to stand up at as many dances as a lady could wish. His legion cannot stay in town long, which is the perfect deterrent to forming a lasting attachment. A word of warning – his low rank means he will not secure an invitation to *all* of society's parties.

The Curate

This gentleman is good, kind and sweet-tempered. However, as the only truly eligible young man within 12 miles of the village, any conversation with him is watched by every expectant mama and her gaggle of daughters.

The Second Son

Far less eligible than his elder brother, but also of easier temper. Will have no wish to marry you unless you have a truly astounding personal fortune.

A LETTER TO ONE WHOM ONCE WAS LOVED

Supplied here is an outline of a model missive one might send to a former suitor, whom one has given every indication of being over. The reader is advised to use only the parts which are applicable, else they run the risk of appearing addlepated.

Sir/Madam/Mx,

I was in raptures upon receiving your charming letter. Please, let us say no more on the subject of you cheating on me/leaving me at the altar/spilling wine over my expensive dress – I assure you I have quite forgotten the matter.

I implore you not to apologize for the length of your letter. It is my chiefest delight to read your many pages on the subject of your unexpected inheritance/ whirlwind romance/successful duel. Just fancy! Such a madcap adventure and you weren't even impoverished by crippling inheritance tax/left broken-hearted as you left me/shot in the arm even a little.

As for my own glad tidings, there is much to say. Alas, I have run out of paper.

Your faithful servant

MAMA'S MATCHMAKING SCHEMES

Darling mothers, who recognize in themselves a genius at arranging both a table and other people's lives, often consider themselves entirely equal to the task of healing their child's heart and arranging their marriage, all in one fell swoop. Aunts, uncles, childhood friends and acquaintances may not escape this accusation – this trait may be found anywhere.

Beware these well-meaning muddlers while you tend to your bruised heart. Listen carefully for mentions of charming fellows, who will no doubt be in attendance on the evening you are invited to dine with them.

When women forget themselves it is never for love of an honest man but of a rascal.

NICOLAS CHAMFORT,
THE CYNIC'S BREVIARY

 A LISTENING EAR

When listening to the account of the varied circumstances that led to two people severing their connection, friends will allow some yardage for embroideries to the tale. Anyone who has a true affection for another person will suspend, temporarily, their knowledge of the sensibility or good nature of the villain of the moment.

While wounded feelings are in play, it is best for the listener to adopt an agreeable disposition. That is, they should agree for now that the former apple of the eye was in fact a sorry wretch, that they should sorely regret their loss and that they should likely never know a moment's peace for the rest of their life.

Later, there will be opportunity to venture that they had *one* or perhaps two good ideas. Time will go on in its healing way and you will both recollect that they were kind, in their way. They may even rejoin your circle. Upon this occasion, any comments made during that first, tear-drenched conversation will of course be forgotten.

*An ill Husband may deprive
a Wife of the Comfort
and Quiet of her Life.*

MARY ASTELL,
*SOME REFLECTIONS
UPON MARRIAGE*

A SECOND CHANCE AT LOVE

Much has been written of the Great First Love. But what of second chances? Is that story not as sweet? To know the bitter taste of lost love and to bite again at the apple – it is brave. Think of all the wisdom you have acquired in the course of the relationship that was not to be brought to fruition. You are so much more aware of which little particularities of character appeal to you in a partner, and which peculiarities you are not able to abide.

A WIT BUT NOT A CYNIC

Disappointment is a great teacher, but don't let her become your master. Love can make people say and do very foolish things, and yet those same people are capable of great kindness and generosity. A disgust in your fellow man, no matter how well founded it seems in your moment of heartbreak, will lead to happiness eluding you. The trick, if you can manage it, is to find humour in the ridiculous and much to pity in the vicious.

Part Three
Proposals and Promises

Loving someone, telling them of your affection, planning for your life together – these should all be undeniably sweet. And yet, the vulnerability that they require cannot help but pluck at the soul. As William Butler Yeats admonished his imagined lover, "Tread softly because you tread on my dreams."

The words that follow are aimed to strengthen your resolve, whether you are offering up your dreams or perhaps preparing to tread just a little on someone else's.

SETTING THE SCENE

One who imagines oneself on the brink of a proposal has a delicate task at hand. One must be alone to receive the offer, for nothing dampens a suitor's ardour more than the presence of a mama, three sisters and a foolish cousin.

Here are some tasks you may set for your inopportune relatives:

Ribbon Shopping

Best suited for: Younger sisters, female cousins. At breakfast, laughingly inform your sister that her dress looks quite unmodish.

Taking to One's Bed

Best suited for: Hypochondriac mamas. Upon spying one's suitor at the door, inform your mama, with utmost sympathy, that she looks a little strained.

Lurking in the Study

Best suited for: Papas. Papas do not generally leave their studies, but it cannot hurt to slip a chair under the door handle until the happy deed is done.

ESCAPING THE SCENE

One who imagines oneself on the brink of an unwelcome proposal has an even more daunting task at hand. One must extricate oneself, with great haste, while causing no undue embarrassment.

Your first and best option is to be quite unavailable. Here are some hints:

Called to the Country

Duration: Three weeks or more. Requires a sympathetic aunt. Must be arranged with some haste, else the proposal will occur before your bags are packed.

The Faint

Duration: Ten minutes. Only to be used on suitors with a mortification of ill-health and a weak sense of feeling.

Locked in the Study (Again)

Duration: Only practical for an afternoon. Your suitor cannot ask for your hand in marriage if they cannot first find your father. However, given most papas' need for victuals and beer, one can only keep them caged for so long.

... *to be sure a love-match was the only thing for happiness, where the parties could any way afford it.*

MARIA EDGEWORTH,
CASTLE RACKRENT

GOTHIC ROMANCE

There is nothing more quelling to a merry mood than to imagine oneself in a romance, only to discover there is more than a touch of gothic in the atmosphere. Before you commit your life, and more importantly your reputation, to just one person, investigate these possible pitfalls:

- ♥ Attics: These should not contain any secret wives. Ideally, neither should the parlour, the breakfast room, the library – or any other room for that matter.
- ♥ Doors: Where possible, these should not creak in an ominous manner.
- ♥ Relatives: Beware older relatives, especially baronets of precarious fortune.
- ♥ Family seats: A person of fortune with a large house is a catch. A person of fortune with a large house set upon a crumbling clifftop should be avoided.

LOVESTRUCK, RAINSWEPT

Two people in love will always encounter each other when caught in a rainstorm. Those in science may theorize that love moves through the body as weather sweeps our earth, and so the two may be uniquely in tune. Thus, two parties, destined for marriage, may meet while they shelter in the pagoda or trip with unruly abandon through the rainswept countryside.

Mamas with a gaggle of daughters and a poorly entailed estate would much rather pledge themselves to chance. The more she sends her pretty daughters out in the rain, the better chance they have of becoming engaged.

The best friend will probably acquire the best wife, because a good marriage is founded on the talent for friendship.

FRIEDRICH NIETZSCHE

Marriage is the best state for a man in general.

SAMUEL JOHNSON

COMPLIMENTS FOR THE WORTHY

Is it not a fine thing to hear pleasant things said about oneself? When one has recovered from the blushes and swoons caused by a well-timed compliment, one should always remember to return the favour. A lover should need no assistance in thinking of their beloved's finer points, but here are some starting ideas to gild their tongue:

- ♥ You write so well – your thumbs move so quickly over the keyboard!
- ♥ How very fine your eyes are.
- ♥ How masterfully you wield your soup spoon!
- ♥ What a wit you are.

GRAND SPEECHES

A word of warning to the suppliant of their loved one's hand in marriage. We offer a word of advice: choose your words with utmost care. A pretty declaration will not turn an unwilling heart to a fond one, but a bungled declaration may certainly reverse that process.

As a suppliant, you should:

- ♥ Make several artful comments regarding the strength and endurance of your love.

- ♥ Comment on the aspects of your loved one's character that first won your affection.

- ♥ Speak to their beauty, although this should never comprise the total of your speech.

As a suppliant, you should not:

- ♥ Remind your loved one of how little you enjoy spending time with their family.
- ♥ Bring the lightness of their purse to their attention.
- ♥ Recall the disagreements that have troubled your conversations, and bring particular attention to the moments in which you were triumphant.

PLACES TO AVOID

Sometimes one is unable to remove oneself entirely from the company of a suitor who has formed an attachment they don't share. On these occasions, be especially cautious in these locations:

Pagoda, Rotunda, Shed

Some suitors are very moved by small garden structures. Those who suspect the dawning of unwelcome romantic feeling in their acquaintance should by no means take a tour of the immediate grounds with them. The merest glimpse of neo-classical architecture and they are likely to make a declaration.

The Library

In the event of being invited to the library by an infatuated suitor, they do *not* need assistance locating a book. In houses populated by many pretty daughters and regular guests, the library can bear witness to many dozens of proposals a year.

A Carriage

It is uncertain whether it is the confined space or limited time that creates such a feeling of urgency within suitors. One can wager that if they enter a carriage with a besotted suitor, they will have received a proposal before they are halfway home.

PREVENTING AN AWKWARD POSITION OF ONE'S OWN MAKING

A deathly silence following an engagement announcement is mortifying. If it occurs at all, one hopes that it is merely the breath before one's assembled loved ones speak in chorus of their congratulations. However, one has, perhaps, led their family to believe that they were on bad terms with their affianced. Words to the effect of "odious", "unbearable" and "unfashionable" may have even crossed their lips. Such is the risk of falling in love with one's enemy.

Heed these wise words and prevent such a situation before it arises:

- ♥ Draw attention to your suitor's kind attentions, no matter how small. Say in elevated tones, "Oh how charming, Mr/Miss/Mx_____ just patted that horse's flank. They are truly kindness personified."
- ♥ Remind everyone of their fortune. If they have none, promote their finest qualities. If that is wit, laugh loudly at the merest joke.
- ♥ Should you fear your family is in no mood to recognize your beloved's good qualities, you must always place them near the family's next-most-despised fiancé/e, in hope they will appear better by comparison.

Love before marriage is absolutely necessary.

SAMUEL RICHARDSON,
PAMELA

PROTECTING YOUR MOTHER'S (AND OTHERS') NERVES

Your announcement must be timed to perfection, whether your mother (or another) welcomes your newly made connection or not.

- ♥ Do not announce at another's engagement party, wedding, baby shower or other significant life event.
- ♥ Do inform your intimate circle before publishing the banns or posting on your socials.
- ♥ Do not reveal the engagement as part of an argument with an odious aunt.
- ♥ Do have a handkerchief on hand to mop up any emotional effusion.

🌿 *BON MOTS* FOR 🌿
YOUR RIVALS IN LOVE

There is no pleasanter company than a rival in love after the battle has been concluded to your satisfaction. Why, one could sit at the window all day, considering different salvos to animate the conversation.

Some samplers:

- ♥ You must feel so rested, my dear, without the burden of planning a wedding.

- ♥ I am quite jealous of your ability to match your jewellery to your garments, while I must wear this engagement ring regardless.

- ♥ You know, I had hardly noticed the handsome stranger in town, being quite preoccupied with my fiancé/e.

Domestic happiness, thou only bliss Of Paradise that has survived the fall!

WILLIAM COWPER

*Marriage follows on love
as smoke on flame.*

NICOLAS CHAMFORT,
A CYNIC'S BREVIARY

THE RIGHT TIME AND NO SOONER

The offer has been made and the happy news shared. All that must be done now is for the date to be set. But this introduces a new dilemma. For how long should you form the engagement?

Marry too quickly and you invite the speculation of the ton/your Instagram followers. Not to say, you may also find yourself at breakfast with someone who is all but a stranger. Wait too long and your fiancé/e may be called to sea, a new heiress may enter society, or a scandalous secret may emerge but moments before you are to be married.

A LETTER TO A SISTER WHO HAS MADE AN ADVANTAGEOUS MATCH

A loyal sister should always share in her sibling's happiness. It follows, then, that she should also share in her good fortune to escape the cloying embrace of her family and the small country village in which she resides.

Dear Sweet Sister,

I am overjoyed to hear that you have returned home from your tour of the continent. How fortunate you are to now be enjoying wedded bliss/as far from this madhouse as possible.

I would by no means intrude on your marital peace. However, given your kind spirit/unpaid dressmaking debt/15 spare bedrooms, I thought you would not refuse a visit from your beloved sibling.

I await your reply with no small amount of impatience. If I have not heard from you in a sennight I will write again/ argue irrevocably with Mama/travel immediately to yours with no intention of leaving.

Yours faithfully,

Your Darling Sibling

Mortified pride in discovering the fallacy of our own judgment; to be ashamed of what we love, yet still to love, are feelings most unpleasant.

SUSAN FERRIER,
MARRIAGE

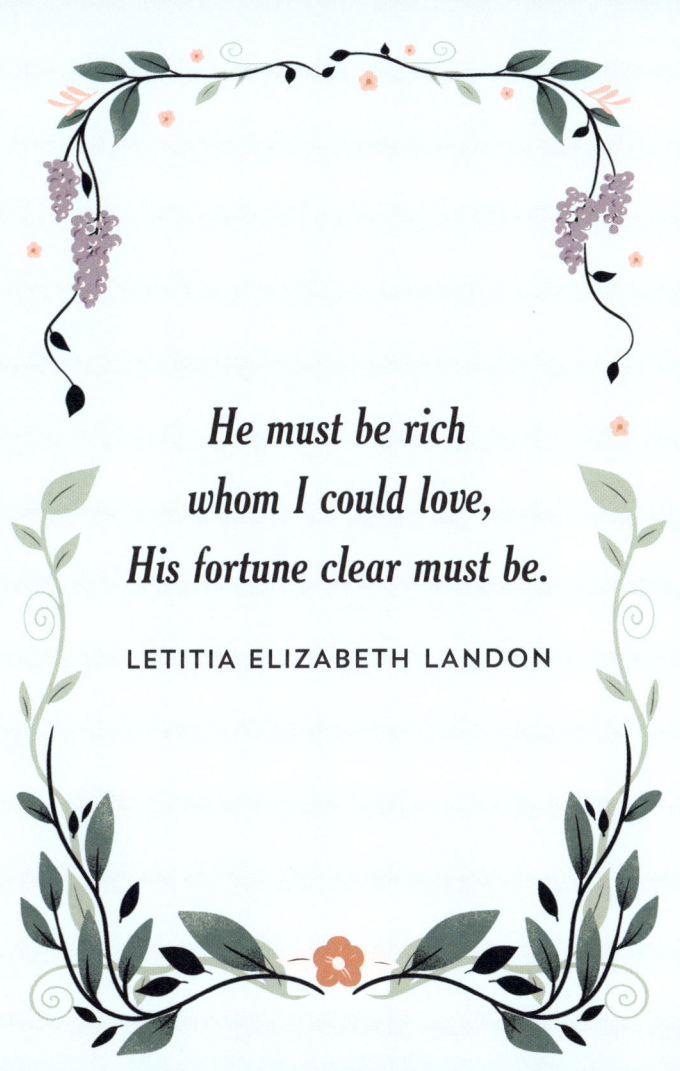

*He must be rich
whom I could love,
His fortune clear must be.*

LETITIA ELIZABETH LANDON

A WOMAN SELDOM ASKS ADVICE BEFORE SHE HAS BOUGHT HER WEDDING CLOTHES.

JOSEPH ADDISON

NEWLYWED FASHIONS

Newlyweds tend to brim with such pleasure in their newfound state that it overflows into every corner of their lives, their family's lives and even the lives of unsuspecting bystanders. Perhaps to achieve these ends, it is the fashion for married Regency ladies to don lace and linen mob caps. Having arrayed herself in her new headwear, acquaintances not apprised of the happy occasion may become joyfully aware. Even the dressmaker, butcher and cheesemonger may find their day much improved by the realization that a *Miss S_____*, whom they meet but thrice a year, has become a *Mrs H_____*.

A COURTSHIP THWARTED

The ton, preoccupied as it is by the marriage mart, has created for itself a new problem to overcome. When two people, each of them fair and eligible, meet and enjoy each other's company very much, there is an obstacle to their becoming fast friends. Each must hint, with utmost delicacy, at the fact they have no romantic interest in the other, without admitting they had the least notion the other might form a romantic attachment. And they must do all this without stumbling on the path to a very welcome friendship.

One might mention, at a natural point in the conversation, that they could only consider matrimony for a sum rather higher than is endowed upon the other. The other may say that they have always been inclined to red hair, knowing they are speaking to a charming blonde. In this manner, the situation gradually reveals itself without either having revealed themselves.

A woman is not to marry a man merely because she is asked.

JANE AUSTEN, *EMMA*

MARRIAGE IS POPULAR BECAUSE IT COMBINES THE MAXIMUM OF TEMPTATION WITH THE MAXIMUM OF OPPORTUNITY.

GEORGE BERNARD SHAW

A TURN ABOUT-FACE

In such a romantic setting as the library, knowing there were a gaggle of interested listeners waiting outside, you said yes. And now, having slept well, eaten well and thought rather long on the matter, you wish to retract that agreement. Your question: can a person, having said yes, then say no?

But of course! There is no circumstance in which an individual cannot break off a connection should their heart no longer belong to the other. Is that not something to be preferred, as the alternative is a life lived and not loved?

A TURN AGAIN ABOUT-FACE

There is a second dilemma for us to consider. Can a person, having said no, then say yes? This is a proposition fraught with a much greater confusion. An individual, having set their heart against someone, may certainly find space for them within it. But they cannot be sure that their own tenancy within that heart is not suspended. All they may do is act on their judgement and share their own developed feelings should they discern that the spurned would welcome the information.

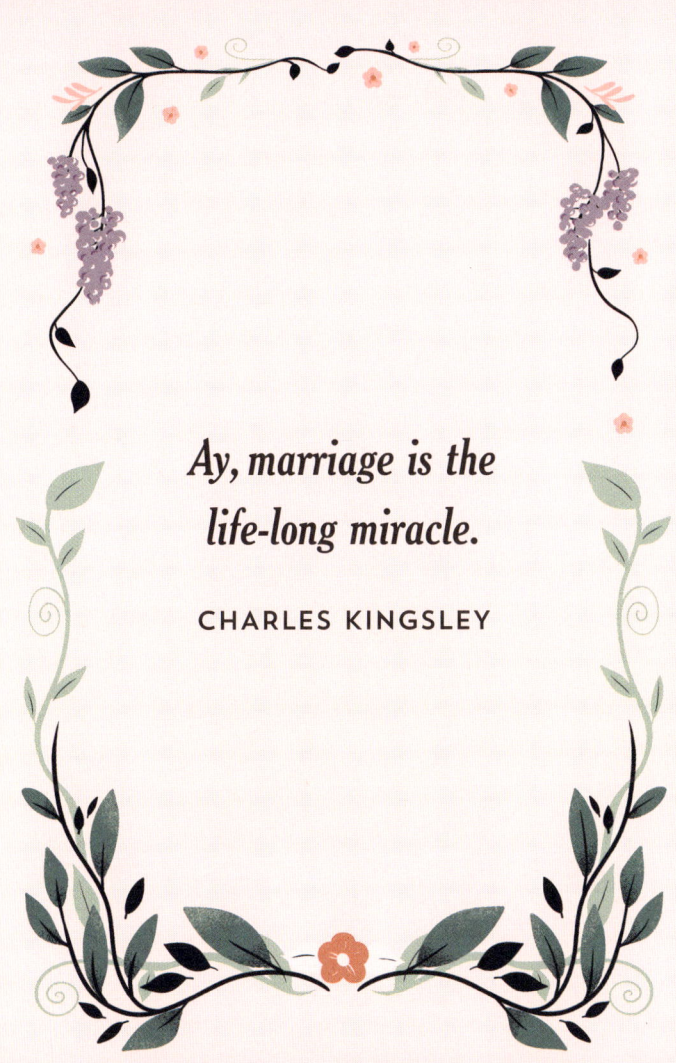

Ay, marriage is the life-long miracle.

CHARLES KINGSLEY

A FLIGHT OF LOVE

After spending a sennight discussing whether to serve white soup at the wedding breakfast, and another debating the flower arrangements, a couple's minds start to wander. An additional glance at the account of the cost and the appeal of a fast horse, a discreet coachman and Gretna Green begins to make itself known. The gatekeepers of the ton hardly dare own it but plenty of elopements have ended in a happy marriage. It is a scandalous start to be sure, but perhaps a provident one.

YOUR MANSION OR MINE?

The decision of where to settle after the wedding is made rather easier when one party still lives with their parents and the other owns a 50-room mansion. Where those obvious differences are not present, a conversation must be had. Consider who wishes to be close to their family, and who, decidedly, does *not*. Should one or other of the couple be in trade or one of the professions, the location of their workplace is inevitably added to the contemplations. Have the conversation early, else the coachman will not know where to go from the wedding and your honeymoon shall be spent in aimless circles around the village.

🌿 STOP THE WEDDING 🌿

In the interest of exorcizing the catastrophic thoughts from your mind, let us consider the reasons a stranger may burst into your wedding and call it to a halt. Assign these reasons a rank from least concerning to most, according to your own considerations:

- ♥ They are married and it is to the milquetoast lady newly arrived in town/it is to a wealthy distant cousin/they have hidden their spouse about the house.

- ♥ *You* are married, although thanks to having one too many glasses of champagne, you do not recall.

- ♥ They are not truly Lord/Lady K_____, they are Lord/Lady K_____'s valet and you are the victim of a con.

- ♥ They have lost everything at cards, including the boots they are wearing.

- ♥ To their embarrassment the intruder has the wrong venue.

- ♥ To *your* embarrassment, you have the wrong venue.

*Love will find its way
Through paths where wolves
would fear to prey.*

**LORD BYRON,
"THE GIAOUR"**

~ FORTUNE ~
FAVOURS THE BOLD

No amount of fluttering a fan in a meaningful fashion, dropping a reticule at the right time or lingering in the library has the impact that a confession has. One may spend one's life dropping the most perfectly crafted hints and reading signs in the way a romantic interest entered the room, but never be certain using these devices. If the dearest reader takes only one piece of advice from these pages, let it be this: tell them how you feel.

CONCLUSION

This book, like many others, closes with a wedding. For a true love story, the wedding is neither the start nor the end of the tale. It is simply a milestone in the journey of love. Now you are equipped with a patience for prigs, a swift comeback for snipes and a ready mind for receiving love. Continue forwards on your journey and walk towards your happiness.

QUOTABLE AUSTEN
Max Morris

ISBN: 978-1-83799-643-8 ♥ Hardback

Celebrate the wit and wisdom of Jane Austen with this charming collection of incisive, entertaining quotes

Still relevant to this day, the wry observations of Jane Austen offer a uniquely humorous perspective on society, relationships, love and money. Bursting with adroit quotes from all her beloved works, this book is a beautifully curated window into the world of this most distinguished writer.

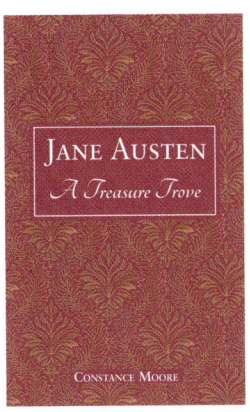

JANE AUSTEN: A TREASURE TROVE
Constance Moore

ISBN: 978-1-83799-645-2 ♥ Hardback

Celebrate the timeless wit and wisdom of Jane Austen with this exquisite collection of classic quotations, fascinating facts and trivia questions that will enchant and inspire. Each page is filled with tart humour, astute observations and the essential truths of love and life, showcasing Austen at her finest.

Have you enjoyed this book? If so, find us on Facebook at Summersdale Publishers, on Twitter/X at @Summersdale and on Instagram, TikTok and Bluesky at @summersdalebooks and get in touch. We'd love to hear from you!

www.summersdale.com

IMAGE CREDITS

Cover art by Alina Bobilova
pp.12, 19 – Regency gentlemen © Vectorbum/Shutterstock.com
pp.39, 49 – letters © zuperia/Shutterstock.com
pp.51, 86 © lemono/Shutterstock.com
p.113 – bonnet © Hanum_Creative/Shutterstock.com
All other illustrations © GoodStudio/Shutterstock.com